BALLET  Is For  EVERYONE

Written by **Rachel Garnet**

ISBN 978-0-578-86744-1 (Hardcover)

Written by Rachel Garnet
www.rachelgarnet.com

Illustrated by Nifty Illustration
www.niftyillustration.com
niftyillustration@mail.com

Dedicated to **Miss Geraldine**

Molly wears a **tutu**,

and her hair up in a **bun**.

She **pirouettes** and **curtsies**.

Ballet is for everyone.

Noah wears a **shirt** and **shorts**.

He likes to **leap** and **run**.

He could **grand jeté** all day.

Ballet is for **everyone**.

Aidan wears a **t-shirt**, too,

and his **tights** with pride and joy.

Aidan likes to **arabesque**. Ballet is for **boys**.

Mia wears her hair in **braids**, that bounce each time she **twirls**.

Her favourite though is her **big bow**.

Ballet is for **girls**.

Logan wears
a **leotard**, and
their **ballet** shoes.

They **grand battement**
with **pointed toes**.

Ballet's for **them** too.

Peter, in his **wheelchair**, shows off his **port de bras.**

 First

Second

Third

Fourth

Ballet is for **all.**

Fifth

Ella wears her **ear muffs**, to **quiet** noisy sounds.

With the music **softer**, Ella's **ballet** bound.

Becca has been **dancing**,

since she was only **three**.

She wants to dance up on the **stage**,

for **everyone** to see.

Michael is a **grandpa**. He's learning from his **son**.

He's not very good yet, but at least he's having **fun**.

The students run out on the **stage**.

They **smile** like the sun.

They're all in this **together**,

because **ballet** is **for everyone**.

Herman is from **Argentina.**

Sylvie is from **France.**

Federico is from **Italy**,

and they all **love to dance**.

Miyako played
a Princess,

Lauren played
a Queen.

Steven played the Fairy King, dressed in leaves of green.

In ballet you can

be a **swan**,

or a **beauty** fast asleep.

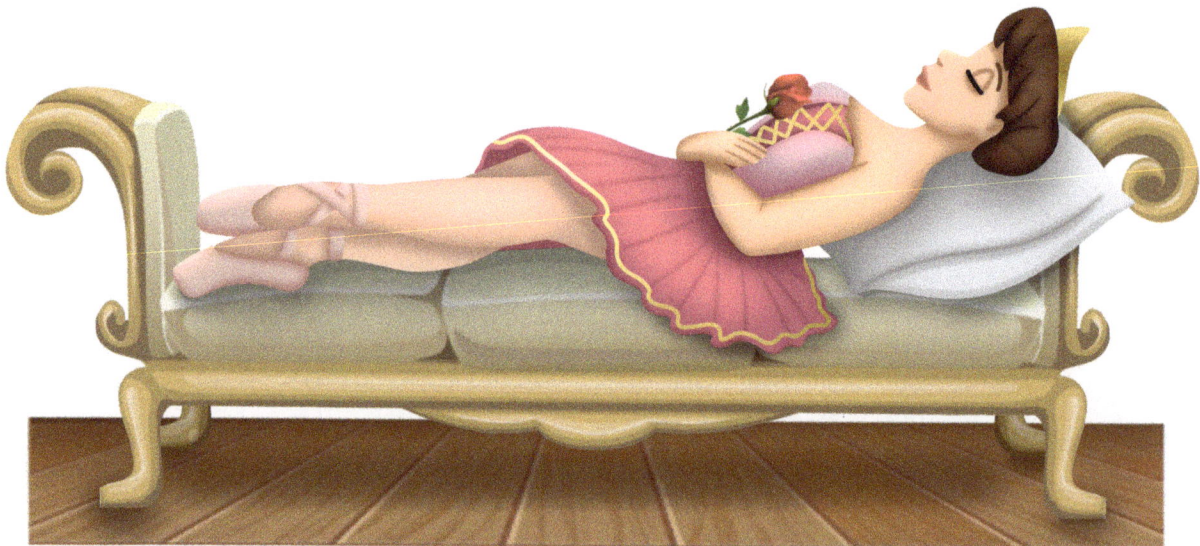

You can be a **king of mice**,

or a **shepherd** herding sheep.

You can be a **diamond**, **emerald**,

ruby, or a **jewel**.

Yes, you can be **anything**,

when you're at **ballet school**.

So now you see that you **can dance**,
if you only **try**.

For when you learn
that **first plié**,

you'll soon learn how to **fly**.

So go and **dance from dusk 'til dawn**.

Your work is never done,

until **everybody**, **everywhere** knows that...

Ballet is for EVERYONE!

About The Book

Ballet is an art that spans **hundreds of years** and in those hundreds of years it hasn't only been girls up on the stage. The stories of ballet feature roles for **all people** no matter their age, gender, or what they look like.

Ballet is for Everyone aims to get anyone and everyone excited about this **art form** that for too long has seemed out of reach and unwelcoming. It is **never too early or too late** to take your first ballet class, and if you've never thought of yourself as a **dancer**, today can be the day you decide you are.

Always remember: You are what a ballet dancer looks like, because ballet is for everyone.

About The Author

Rachel fell in love with ballet when she was 14 years old, but when she started taking class, she was told that she was too old to ever be able to catch up. This didn't stop Rachel and she kept dancing. Taking class with students 5 years younger than herself, Rachel slowly built up her skills and let her love of ballet drive her forward. When Rachel moved to Vancouver, Canada, she began studying ballet through the Royal Academy of Dance. There, she felt supported by teachers who didn't care about her age and just wanted to foster her passion. Today, Rachel is an ABT® Certified Teacher, who has successfully completed the ABT® Teacher Training Intensive in Pre-Primary through Level 3 of the ABT® National Training Curriculum. She also holds a Certificate of Advanced Foundation from the Royal Academy of Dance. She has been teaching children in both the US and Canada that ballet is for everyone!

Basic Ballet Terms

Pirouette: When a dancer does a turn on one leg.
You can see Molly doing a pirouette.

Grand Jeté: When a dancer does a big leap.
You can see Noah do a grand jeté.

Arabesque: When a dancer lifts their leg straight up.
You can see Aidan do an arabesque.

Grand Battement: When a dancer does a big kick.
You can see Logan do a grand battement.

Port de Bras: When a dancer does one of the 5 classical positions that dancers hold their arms in.
You can see Peter doing the positions of the port de bras.

Plié: When a dancer bends their legs. This is often the first ballet move a dancer learns and is the one that is used most often.
You can see Michael doing a plié.

Tendu: When a dancer straightens their leg out from the body while keeping their pointed toes still touching the ground.
You can see Steven showing off his tendu.

Exciting Moments In Ballet History

- **1400s Italy** - A dance style that will eventually become ballet begins to gain popularity in the Royal Court of Italy.

- **1650s France** - King Louis XIV of France popularises ballet in the French Royal Court. He dances many roles during his reign. He also establishes a dance school.

- **1832 France** - La Sylphide premieres at the Paris Opera Ballet, choreographed by Filippo Taglioni. Ballerina Marie Taglioni dances the role of the Sylph en pointe.

- **1877 Russia** - Swan Lake premieres at the Bolshoi Ballet, choreographed by Julius Reisinger.

Exciting Moments In Ballet History

- **1913 France** - The Rite of Spring is first performed by the Ballets Russes. The performance's strange music and contemporary style cause mass panic.

- **1920-1960** - Ballet companies open across the world during this period including
The Royal Ballet in England, The Colon Theater Ballet in Argentina, Cairo Opera Ballet Company in Egypt, and the American Ballet Theatre in the USA.

- **1974 USA** - An all-male ballet company called Les Ballets Trockadero de Monte Carlo does their first performance.

- **Today** - You show off your ballet skills and prove that ballet is for everyone.

9 780578 867441